Presented by:

_____

To:

_____

Date:

_____

Occasion:

_____

W9-BGK-163

On Our
Pilgrimage to Eternity

"99 Words to Live By"

A series of fine gift books that presents inspirational words by renowned authors and captivating thinkers. Thought-provoking proverbs from many peoples and traditions complete each volume's collection.

"99 Words to Live By" explores topics that have moved and will continue to move people's hearts. Perfect for daily reflection as well as moments of relaxation.

On Our
Pilgrimage to Eternity

99 Sayings
by John Paul II

edited by
Stephen Liesenfeld

NCP
New City Press

Published in the United States by New City Press
202 Cardinal Rd., Hyde Park, NY 12538
©2004 New City Press (English translation)

Translated by Eugene Selzer
from the original German edition
Gott steht auf der Seite des Menschen
©2003 Verlag Neue Stadt, Munich.

Cover picture: Neue Stadt Archives

Paperback edition (May 2005): ISBN 1-56548-230-1

Library of Congress Cataloging-in-Publication Data:

John Paul II, Pope, 1920-
  [Selections. English. 2004]
On Our Pilgrimage to Eternity: 99 sayings / by John Paul II ;
  edited by Stephen Liesenfeld ; [translated by Gene Selzer].
      p. cm. -- (99 words to live by)
    ISBN 1-56548-198-4
    1. John Paul II, Pope, 1920--Quotations. 2. Christian
life--Quotations, maxims, etc. 3. Christian life--Catholic
authors. I. Liesenfeld, Stephen. II Title. III. Series.

BX1378.5.J656A25   2004
242--dc22   2003063529

Printed in Canada

When Karol Wojtyla succeeded Albino Luciani, the "pope of 33 days," who could possibly have foreseen the consequences? In the words of David Brooks, "Pope John Paul II . . . has had a more profound influence on more people than any other living human being" (*The New York Times*, October 11, 2003). The pontificate of the first non-Italian since the sixteenth century indeed has left a lasting imprint on the church and on the world.

As the world has faced the tremendous theological, social, economic and political realignment of the last half of the twentieth century, Pope John Paul II has offered clear guidance not only for Roman Catholics and Christians of other denominations but also for members of other great religions and all people of good will. He has promoted ecumenism and interreligious dialogue, especially with Jews and Muslims. With tireless eloquence, he has called out for peace. Beginning during his tenure as cardinal archbishop of Krakow, he has helped to engineer the fall of the "iron curtain" and to fill the vacuum left by the fall of Communism with a new society based on Christian principles.

A basic motif runs through the life and work of Karol Wojtyla. He centers his thought directly on the human person — not humanity in the abstract but the person as an existential reality — in every dimension, embracing our deepest desires and concrete needs for work and food, for worth and respect, with opportunities for our cultural and artistic development. Human rights, human worth, the richness of human culture, the dignity of those who suffer, religious freedom, justice and peace

— these recurring themes weave through the speeches and writings of Pope John Paul II. They well from within his own experience: living under two very different totalitarian systems; sharing friendship with a young Jewish companion during his schooldays; engaging in artistic productions, especially literature and theater; never retreating from grievous suffering, especially the assassination attempt of 1981 and his progressive illness. Each event has left a lasting mark.

The good news of Jesus, humanity's friend and savior, is relevant to our own life and times: that is the central creed of this defender of the human person. The following brief selections from his writings should make this evident.

Stephen Liesenfeld

There is only one true measure of the human spirit, and it is love.

You cannot live
without love.
To do so would leave you
without self-understanding.
If you do not discover, receive
and make love your own
by embracing it
in ample life-giving measure,
then your life
is devoid of meaning.

People are to be affirmed
for their own sake.
For their own sake alone!
To go even further:
we must love them
simply because
they are human persons.
Love needs no other reason
than the inestimable dignity
of every individual.

We do justice
to others
when we love them. . . .
Love for others
precludes using them
as objects.

Profound esteem
for human worth
and dignity
is also known as
Good News, Gospel.

No one can be forced to accept the truth.

But our very nature, which is rooted in freedom, already compels us to seek out the truth.

The starting point for "missionary" effort must be our attitude of reverence for the very essence of human nature" (John 2:25), a reverence for what is present in our innermost being concerning life's deepest and weightiest problems; it is reverence for the inner working of the Spirit, who "blows where it will" (John 3:8).

Whenever one lives right-
eously and searches honestly
for the truth, with a readiness to
accept it when found, then the
gospel is already at work in the
subconscious, even though
one may not yet be aware of it
or may even deliberately reject
it. For openness to the truth
presupposes that grace is
already operative within. The
Spirit blows when and where it
will.

What is at stake is the human person — human persons in their full reality, in their total dimension — not "abstract" persons, but real, "concrete" and "historical" persons. This includes every "individual" person; for the mystery of salvation touches each and every one, and Christ is forever linked to each one of us in this mystery.

"Dominion"
over the visible world,
as the creator
entrusted it to us means:
the priority of ethics
over technology,
the primacy of people
over things,
and the preeminence
of spirit over matter.

It is not a matter
of *"having* more"
but of *"being"* more.

There is a real danger that with enormous progress in mastering the outer world we abandon the essential fabric of our inner world. We ourselves can become the objects of gross, often imperceptible manipulation — through social organization, systems of production and the public media.

We cannot abdicate
our role in the world.
We must not become
slaves of things,
slaves of economic systems,
slaves of production,
slaves of our own creations.
A civilization that assumes a
purely material character
would condemn us
to that kind of slavery.

We must consider the dangerous consequences of unrestricted development. We must not do all that we are capable of doing. Asceticism, self-control, self-denial — all these ancient strategies — have taken on a surprisingly new relevance and become fashionable; indeed, they have become essential for human survival.

As we look at the created world we realize that we have it only on loan. It comes to us as God's gift, and eventually we must return this gift to him. We have no right to turn it into an ecological wilderness, or to destroy it.

How can we stand on the sidelines when we are facing an ecological catastrophe capable of rendering vast areas of our planet infertile and uninhabitable?

How can we ignore the menacing nightmare of catastrophic war that constantly threatens peace?

How can we dismiss widespread contempt for the human rights of so many persons, especially children?

Today we sense more than ever a pressing need for solidarity as a basic prerequisite for all joint international efforts. We realize that the goods the creator entrusted to us are intended for all.

Without solidarity
there is no freedom.

Freedom always comes at a high price. It requires a generous heart, ready for sacrifice. . . . We cannot excuse ourselves from our own personal responsibility for freedom. There is no such thing as freedom without sacrifice.

Those who are ready to follow the path of freedom do not identify opponents with the error they hold. On the contrary, they look at the error objectively and appeal to the others' reason, to their heart and conscience, so as to help them find and acknowledge the truth.

There is no freedom
without peoples'
readiness for open
and ongoing dialogue.

Dialogue paves the way to truth. It provides an indispensable means to freedom. Truth never fears honorable agreement, since such concord brings along with it the light that allows one to advocate truth without abandoning convictions and essential values. Truth brings souls together; it shines light on what already unites those who had been divided; it casts aside mistrust of the past and prepares the ground for continuing progress in justice and fraternity so that all can live together in peace.

All who lovingly and respectfully seek the truth and proclaim it before others are working for peace. The same can be said for those who extend themselves to show their esteem for the language of different cultures, for the uniqueness of individual nations, and for the rich human values in every people. . . . Almost every area of human activity offers opportunities for building freedom. . . . When words fail and diplomacy is uncertain, people can find accord through music, art, theater and sport.

To know love
is to know freedom.

Love lets us go
beyond ourselves
and sets us free
through our concern
for others
and our desire
for their success.

Christians become
"salt of the earth" and
"light of the world" (Mt 5:13f)
when they learn how to bring
truly human qualities
to their work by doing it
out of love for God
and in a spirit
of service to others.

In our work and in economic matters we must always maintain a reflective attitude. With all due integrity we must safeguard the undeniable worth of the human person , not just for workers themselves but also for their families; not only for people today but also for generations to come.

The charge to earn our bread by the sweat of our brow is also a right. If a society systematically denies this right and does not take the appropriate political and economic measures to make work available to laborers by establishing a satisfactory base for employment, then it cannot justify itself morally nor can it ever reach a just social accord.

Work is more than a way to make a living. It is a dimension of human existence. It can and must be sanctified, so that people can realize their true vocation as creatures made in God's image and likeness.

* * *

All honorable work deserves respect.

God is always
standing on the side
of those who suffer.

The world
of human suffering
ceaselessly evokes
another world:
the world of human love.

When disinterested love
is awakened
in the human heart
and moves into action,
this is due in a certain sense
to suffering. . . .
One cannot remain indifferent
to the suffering of others.
It makes one pause,
agonize and act.

We must not remain indifferent to the lot of other members of the human family, as though this has nothing to do with us.

No one can claim lack of responsibility for the fate of a brother or sister.

It is time for a new "vision of love" that involves not just the offering of assistance, but rather the ability to make oneself neighbor to those who are suffering. We must become one with them, so that they perceive our assistance not as humiliating condescension but as fraternal sharing.

Institutions are important and indispensable; but none of them can replace the compassion, love, and initiative that comes from the human heart, when we address the suffering of others. That applies to physical suffering, but even more to the anguish of the spirit.

Christ says: "You have done it to me." He is present in each one who receives our love; he is the one who welcomes our help. . . . He is present in those who suffer. . . .

Christ has taught us both to accomplish good through suffering and to do good to those who are suffering. In these two ways he has disclosed the full meaning of suffering.

God's almighty power is revealed in the very fact that he has freely accepted suffering. He did not need to do that. . . .

Yet Jesus persevered on the cross; he could say with all who suffer: "My God, my God, why have you forsaken me?" (Mk 15:34). This has stood throughout human history as reason to persevere. If there had been no fight to the finish on the cross, the truth that God is love would have vanished into thin air.

Yes, God is love, and that is why he has given his son, that he might reveal God's unending love. Christ "has loved his own to the end" (John 13:1). . . . The Man of Sorrows is the revelation of a love that "endures all" (1 Cor 13:7), for "the greatest of these is love" (cf. 1 Cor 13:13).

Christ has manifested his love through his suffering and death, and his suffering and death continue in those he so deeply loves: he lives in them. . . . It is primarily through the cross that he continues to identify with us.

Sickness is truly a cross and at times it is a heavy one. It is a visitation that God permits in our lives, part of an unfathomable mystery that exceeds our understanding.

We should not look upon illness as blind chance, and we can be sure it never comes as a punishment. It never ravages without leaving behind something positive.

The cross of suffering weighs heavily on the body. But when it is carried in union with the cross of Christ it becomes a source of redemption, life and resurrection for the one who is suffering, for others and even for all humanity.

Healing involves
embracing and accepting
another with redeeming love:
a love that is mightier
than any sin could be.

There have been times when Christians added page after page to the history of intolerance. In not following the great commandment of love they have distorted the face of the church. . . . Christians have often betrayed the gospel and yielded to the rule of force. They have trampled the rights of peoples and nations, with contempt for their culture and religious traditions:

Lord, grant us pardon and forgiveness! Have mercy on us!

Christian holiness does not consist in being free from sin but in seeking to fall as few times as possible and then rising again after each fall. This is not so much the fruit of human will power; rather, it is the result not of resisting, but of cooperating humbly with the grace in our hearts.

The kingdom of God
is open not to those
who are great dignitaries,
but to those
who are poor in spirit.

In the cross
and resurrection of his Son
God has embraced
all of humanity.

The right to life is a fundamental human right. . . . No other right touches human existence so directly! The right to life means the right to enter the world and continue in it until natural death: "As long as I live, I have the right to live."

Human life is fundamentally inviolate; and since the unborn child does not first become human later, but is human from the moment of conception, there is no initial period in which that child can be treated as disposable.

Dying persons do not want
to be abandoned to pills
so much as they want
hope, human contact and
someone to hold their hand.

In love we find
the key to all hope,
for true love has its roots
in God himself.

A family cannot live, grow and develop as a community of persons without true mutual love; for it is love that brings the gift of life to children and leads to rapport and communion with other families.

In order to love
with a genuine love
we must be freed
of many things
and above all
from ourselves;
to love truly
means to give freely
"without expectation"
— and to love to the end.

God's word stands,
even when human words fail.
God's word holds fast,
even if the human speaker
proves false.
So we pray with the psalmist:
"Before dawn I come
and cry out.
I hope in your words."

The cross and resurrection
of Christ are mightier
than any distress
and evil we may fear.

To be delivered in our day from fear of self, of the world, of others, of earthly powers, of oppression . . . we can only recommend cultivating in our hearts a true fear of the Lord, for that has always been the beginning of wisdom.

Fear of the Lord produces people who are guided by responsibility and by dutiful love.

Perhaps more than ever
we need to hear the word
of the risen Christ:
"Be not afraid!"

There must grow in the consciousness of all peoples and nations the awareness that there is someone who holds in his hand the destiny of this passing world . . . someone who is the Alpha and Omega of every individual and of all human history. This someone is love: incarnate love, crucified and risen love! It is love unfailingly present among us. It is eucharistic love, the abiding source of community. Only the one who embodies this love can say with fully guaranteed assurance: "Be not afraid!"

"Be not afraid!" God is with us. The God of absolute holiness is not just *with* us, he has become flesh in Jesus Christ. So be not afraid before the God-made-man! Be not afraid before the divine mystery; have no fear in the presence of his love; have no fear before human frailty nor before human grandeur! Even in weakness, humanity does not cease to be great. Be not afraid to give witness to the dignity of every person from the moment of conception till the moment of death!

Even though our faith in the fundamental dignity of the human person may be shaken and threatened, and long-held positions and convictions may have hardened our hearts, there is yet a power that overwhelms all deep-seated mistrust, suspicion, or resentment; it is Jesus Christ, who has brought forgiveness and reconciliation to the world.

To be a child of God
means to make room
for the Holy Spirit,
to follow his lead
and remain open
to his action
in our own lives
and in the world.

People who make history are those who are deeply convinced of the human vocation: the call to search, to struggle and to create.

Is it better to be satisfied with a life without ideals, content with a society characterized by indifference, ruthlessness and pride, or to pursue a generous search for truth, goodness and justice, and work for a world that reflects the beauty of God — even though this prize will be achieved only through much affliction?

The quality of our decisions will be measured in those difficult moments, the moments of testing. There is no shortcut to light and glory!

The person of faith has caught sight of the lighthouse that guides our voyage. A believer has a direction, an orientation. . . . One who believes has a focal point and knows how to live a life that is worthy and God-pleasing. People of faith will be able finally to lay down their lives with full awareness and say yes when God issues his final summons.

God is joy
and in life's joys
we find the reflection
of that original joy
which filled God
when he created us.

* * *

Christianity is joy,
and whoever professes it
should radiate this joy
by passing it on
and spreading it everywhere.

The gospel does not
promise easy success.
It does not promise
a tranquil life.
It makes demands,
yet leads to
a glorious inheritance.

The gospel embraces a fundamental paradox:
We must lose life in order
    to find it;
we must die in order to live;
we must take up the cross if we
    want to be saved.
This is the basic truth of the
gospel, yet we continue to rebel
against it.

The "evangelical" witness that the world accepts most readily is concern for others and love for the poor, the lowly and the suffering.

Once we are inserted into the "today" of Jesus Christ there is no longer any danger that we will revert to "yesterdays." Christ is the measure of time. In his divine-human "today" the clash between "traditional" and "progressive" is healed at the source.

Often we sense an inner emptiness; we feel sad and discontented. We may have everything, but we live without joy. It is especially disconcerting to see around us so much suffering, so much distress, misery and violence. Yet precisely in this tragedy of human existence, into this very human drama there sounds the eternal message of the gospel: Jesus loves you! Jesus has come into the world as the confirmation of God's love. He has come to love us and to be loved by us. Let Christ love you!

Christians cannot lead a double life: a so-called "spiritual" life with its values and expectations on the one side — and a so-called "worldly" life involving family, work, social relationships, political and cultural concerns on the other. . . .

Every deed, every situation, every concrete duty — such as competence and cooperation at work, love and devotion in the family . . . social and political service . . . — all are opportunities to practice faith, hope and love.

What we do
must always be in tune
with what we believe.

We cannot base our lives today on the glory of our Christian past. Our oneness with Christ in the eucharist must be evident in our daily lives here and now — in our actions, in our conduct, in our lifestyle, in our relationships with others.

One cannot
"toy with living."
One cannot
"play around with dying."
And one cannot
"dabble in loving."

The great task before us is to make the church a home base and a school for communion. Even before launching great enterprises we need a *spirituality of communion*. . . . Among other things, that means recognizing others as my own concern by sharing their joy and their sorrow, sensing their wants, embracing their needs, and finally offering a deep and genuine friendship.

A spirituality of communion requires the ability to see what is positive in others, accepting and cherishing them as a gift of God. What I give to others becomes not just a gift for them; it turns out to be also a gift for myself.

The spirituality of communion ultimately means "making room" for others by "bearing one another's burdens" (Gal 6:2). It demands that we resist the temptation of egoism that continually threatens to produce rivalry, selfish attachment to one's own career, mistrust and jealousy.

There can be no worthy community without deep regard for transcendent and lasting values. If we measure the universe only in terms of ourselves, without reference to its true origin and purpose, we soon become slaves of our own priorities.

No more war!
No more devastation!

We can no longer tolerate a situation that produces nothing but the fruits of death: murder, destroyed cities, collapsed economies, hospitals without medicines, sick and elderly left to themselves, families rent asunder in grief.

Peace is possible, if we recognize that cultural values must prevail over claims of race or power.

It is urgent to develop a culture of peace — stimulated by sentiments of tolerance and universal cooperation. Without such a culture of peace, war will continue to lurk in the background and smolder under the embers of an uncertain truce.

Whoever cannot live
in peace with God
can hardly live in peace
with brother and sister.

The ethical progress of a society reveals itself in the degree to which minorities participate in the political process.

* * *

Discriminating against people because of their religious convictions is a fundamental injustice against God and humanity. Whenever that happens, we seal ourselves off from the road to peace.

If you know the joy
of praying, you know
that the experience cannot
be expressed in words.
The only possible way
to discover the hidden
richness of prayer
is by praying.
You learn to pray
by doing it.

Prayer brings us the strength to live the great ideal. . . . Prayer brings the courage to rise again from indifference and guilt, if one is unfortunate enough to be crushed under temptation and weakness. Prayer brings the light to see the events of one's own life and of history from God's perspective.

The fundamental unity of the human race is founded upon its origin in God the creator. No one group has the right to place itself above another. The world needs mutual regard based on true solidarity free of discrimination. Therefore the state has the duty to respect the differences in its citizens and direct these differences toward the common good.

Why has the God of holiness permitted such division among Christians? A negative answer would explain the loss of Christian unity as the bitter fruit of Christian sinfulness. But a more positive view would invite us to trust in the one who can wrest good even out of evil and out of human weakness: Perhaps these divisions now provide an opportunity for the church to discover the full riches of the redemptive gospel of Christ; for otherwise these riches might never have come to light.

The will of Christ
compels us
to strive earnestly
and resolutely
toward unity
with all our Christian
brothers and sisters.
In the process
we become aware
that the desired unity
requires a perfect faith
that combines
truth and love.

The ecumenical path
is tiring and perhaps
lengthy,
yet we are heartened
by our faith in the risen Christ
who leads us and in
the inexhaustible power
of his Spirit who continues
to surprise us anew.

The church is guided
by its certain faith
that in Jesus Christ
the Creator is accomplishing
the work of salvation.

* * *

God desires the salvation
of all, and he presents himself
to each one of us
in a mysterious
but real way.

We should not be surprised that providence has allowed so many different religions; we should rather be surprised that they embrace so many common elements.

All humanity
is a single family,
for all are created
in the image of God.
All have a
common destination,
as they are called
to find in God
the complete fulfillment
of their lives.
Despite differences of faith,
as Christians are
especially aware all are
engulfed
in a mystery of unity.

90

In the synagogue of Rome

For us the Jewish religion is not something "extraneous"; rather it resides in a certain way within the "core" of our Christian faith. We have a relationship unlike that between any other religions.
You are our cherished brothers and, let us say, our elder brothers.

Jews and Christians are called as children of Abraham to be a blessing for the world (cf. Gen 12:2f) by working together for freedom and justice for everyone, and to do it to the extent God intends, by being ready to sacrifice ourselves in whatever way this exalted purpose may require.

To the Islamic Community

I share your faith that humanity owes its existence to a merciful God, the creator of heaven and earth. In a world where many reject or ignore God, a world so full of suffering and in need of God's mercy, we must work together as courageous bearers of hope.

To the Buddhist Community

I have the deepest respect for your way of life, based as it is on compassion and loving kindness, and on the desire for freedom, well-being and harmony among all creatures.

May we all give witness to this compassion and benevolence by striving to promote the genuine welfare of all.

To the Hindu Community

I have high regard for your search for interior peace, and for a world peace that does not operate out of purely mechanistic or materialistic political considerations, but is based on individual purification, selflessness, love and compassion for all. May every human heart be transformed by such love and understanding.

The interreligious dialogue must continue. In the 21st century we foresee an increasing cultural and religious pluralism in society. Dialogue is essential in this situation, to assure a stronger foundation for peace and to banish the grim specter of religious wars, which have stained so many generations of human history with blood. God is one and his name which is one constrains us to seek peace and harmony.

What we need
is a new paradigm
for living.

A paradigm for living means respect for nature and care for the creator's handiwork. That means especially respect for human life. A paradigm for living means serving the under-privileged, the poor and oppressed; justice and freedom are inseparable: they exist only if they exist *for all*.

A paradigm for living
involves thanking God
each day for the gift of life,
for our own worth
and dignity as human beings,
and for the friendship
that he offers us
on our pilgrimage
to eternity.

Sources:

Encyclicals:
Redemptor hominis
Centesimus annus
Salvifici doloris
Novo millennio ineunte

Spalancate le porte a Cristo (Open the doors to Christ), Milan 1990.

Die Schwelle der Hoffnung überschreiten (Crossing the Threshold of Hope), Hamburg 1994.

Orientierung für das dritte Jahrtausend (Guideposts for the third millennium), Graz-Wien-Köln 1997.

Also available now:

The Golden Thread of Life
99 Sayings on Love
ISBN 1-56548-182-8, 112 pp., hardcover

Blessed Are
the Peacemakers
99 Sayings on Peace
ISBN 1-56548-183-6, 112 pp., hardcover

Sunshine On Our Way
99 Sayings on Friendship
ISBN 1-56548-195-X, 112 pp., hardcover

Organizations and Corporations

This title is available at special quantity discounts for bulk purchases for sales promotions, premiums, or fundraising.
For information call or write:

New City Press, Marketing Dept.
202 Cardinal Rd.
Hyde Park, NY 12538.
Tel: 1-800-462-5980;
1-845-229-0335
Fax: 1-845-229-0351
info@newcitypress.com